The Word Party

The Word Party

RICHARD EDWARDS

Illustrated by John Lawrence

LUTTERWORTH PRESS

CAMBRIDGE

LUTTERWORTH PRESS
7 All Saints' Passage
Cambridge CB2 3LS

Text copyright © 1986 Richard Edwards
Illustrations copyright © 1986 John Lawrence

British Library Cataloguing in Publication Data

Edwards, Richard, *1949–*
    Word party,
    I. Title II. Lawrence, John, *1933–*
    821'.914   PZ8.3

ISBN 0–7188–2649–3

First published 1986

Printed in Great Britain at The Bath Press, Avon

Contents

7 *When I Was Three*

8 *Snow*

10 *Littlemouse*

12 *The Number*

13 *The Word Party*

14 *Our Pond*

16 *Don't*

17 *Badgers*

19 *Monster*

20 *Mr Marrumpeter's Shop*

22 *The Rainflower*

24 *Two Friends*

25 *Susannah*

26 *Uncle Ted's Tea*

28 *Cloudburst*

30 *Gypsy Jill*

32 *A Wild One*

34 *To Slim or Not to Slim*

35 *My Dear Salooma*

36 *If Only*

37 *How?*

A Corner of Bread 39

Can You Help? 40

A Song without Music
   or Very Much Sense 41

The Wind 42

It 44

Three Owls 45

Wizard 47

The Blue Room 48

Be Careful 49

The Mandradum 50

George Mackenzie 52

Say This as Fast as You Can 54

Cooking 55

At Midnight 56

The Rippling River 58

My Little Dog 60

The Door 61

A Forest by Night 62

The Song of a Mole 64

When I Was Three

When I was three I had a friend
Who asked me why bananas bend,
I told him why, but now I'm four
I'm not so sure. . . .

Snow

I've just woken up and I'm lying in bed
With the end of a dream going round in my head,
And something much quieter and softer than rain
Is brushing the window pane.

It's snowing! It's snowing! My room's filled with light.
Outside it's like Switzerland, everything's white.
That bulge is our dustbin, that hummock's the wall.
I can't see the flower-beds at all.

I've got to get out there. I've got to get dressed.
I can't find my pants and I can't find my vest.
Who's taken my jumper? Who's hidden my belt?
It might be beginning to melt!

I'm outside. I'm running. I'm up to my waist.
I'm rolling. I'm tasting the metally taste.
There's snow down my trousers and snow up my nose.
I can't even feel my toes.

I'm tracking a polar bear over the ice,
I'm making a snow-man, he's fallen down twice,
I'm cutting some steps to the top of the hedge,
Tomorrow I'm building a sledge.

I'm lying in bed again, tucked up tight;
I know I'll sleep soundly and safely tonight.
My snow-man's on guard and his shiny black eyes
Are keeping a look-out for spies.

Sleep quietly, sleep deeply, sleep calmly, sleep curled
In warm woolly blankets while out in the world,
On field and forest and mountain and town
The snow flakes like feathers float down.

Littlemouse

Light of day going,
Harvest moon glowing,
People beginning to snore,
Tawny owl calling,
Dead of night falling,
Littlemouse opening her door.

Scrabbling and tripping,
Sliding and slipping,
Over the ruts of the plough,
Under the field gate,
Mustn't arrive late,
Littlemouse hurrying now.

Into a clearing,
All the birds cheering,
Woodpecker blowing a horn,
Nightingale fluting,
Blackbird toot-tooting,
Littlemouse dancing till dawn.

Soon comes the morning,
No time for yawning,
Home again Littlemouse creeps,
Over the furrow,
Back to her burrow,
Into bed. Littlemouse sleeps.

The Number

There is a magic number
And if you say it standing on your head,
Your dreams will all come true,
Your old things will be new,
You'll never cry
Or sit alone and sigh.

I found it out by chance
While upside down against the garden shed.
I can't give it away,
I'm not allowed to say,
But here's a clue:
It isn't sixty-two.

The Word Party

Loving words clutch crimson roses,
Rude words sniff and pick their noses,
Sly words come dressed up as foxes,
Short words stand on cardboard boxes,
Common words tell jokes and gabble,
Complicated words play Scrabble,
Swear words stamp around and shout,
Hard words stare each other out,
Foreign words look lost and shrug,
Careless words trip on the rug,
Long words slouch with stooping shoulders,
Code words carry secret folders,
Silly words flick rubber bands,
Hyphenated words hold hands,
Strong words show off, bending metal,
Sweet words call each other "petal",
Small words yawn and suck their thumbs
Till at last the morning comes.
Kind words give out farewell posies . . .

Snap! The dictionary closes.

Our Pond

The pond in our garden
Is murky and deep
And lots of things live there
That slither and creep,

Like diving bell spiders
And great ramshorn snails
And whirligig beetles
And black snappertails.

There used to be goldfish
That nibbled my thumb,
But now there's just algae
And sour, crusty scum.

There used to be pondweed
With fizzy green shoots,
But now there are leeches
And horrible newts.

One day when my football
Rolled in by mistake
I tried to retrieve it
By using a rake,

But as I leaned over
A shape from the ooze
Bulged up like a nightmare
And lunged at my shoes.

I ran back in shouting,
But everyone laughed
And said I was teasing
Or else I was daft.

But I know what happened
And when I'm asleep
I dream of those creatures
That slither and creep:

The diving bell spiders
And great ramshorn snails
And whirligig beetles
And black snappertails.

Don't

Why do people say "don't" so much,
Whenever you try something new?
It's more fun doing than don'ting,
So why don't people say "do"?

Don't slurp your spaghetti
Don't kiss that cat
Don't butter your fingers
Don't walk like that
Don't wash your books
Don't bubble your tea
Don't jump on your sister
Don't goggle at me
Don't climb up the curtains
Don't feed the chair
Don't sleep in your wardrobe
Don't cut off your hair
Don't draw on the pillow
Don't change all the clocks
Don't water the phone
Don't hide my socks
Don't cycle upstairs
Don't write on the eggs
Don't chew your pajamas
Don't paint your legs. . .

Oh, why do people say "don't" so much,
Whenever you try something new?
It's more fun doing than don'ting,
So why don't people say "do"?

Badgers

Badgers come creeping from dark under ground,
Badgers scratch hard with a bristly sound,
Badgers go nosing around.

Badgers have whiskers and black and white faces,
Badger cubs scramble and scrap and run races,
Badgers like overgrown places.

Badgers don't jump when a vixen screams,
Badgers drink quietly from moonshiny streams,
Badgers dig holes in our dreams.

Badgers are working while you and I sleep,
Pushing their tunnels down twisting and steep,
Badgers have secrets to keep.

Monster

I saw a monster in the woods
As I was cycling by,
His footsteps smouldered in the leaves,
His breath made bushes die,

And when he raised his hairy arm
It blotted out the sun;
He snatched a pigeon from the sky
And swallowed it in one.

His mouth was like a dripping cave,
His eyes like pools of lead,
And when he growled I rode back home
And rushed upstairs to bed.

But that was yesterday and though
It gave me quite a fright,
I'm older now and braver so
I'm going back tonight.

I'll tie him up when he's asleep
And take him to the zoo.
The trouble is he's rather big . . .
Will you come too?

Mr Marrumpeter's Shop

In Mr Marrumpeter's junk shop
There is a peculiar clock,
It always strikes four
When you go in the door,
It sometimes says tick but it never says tock
In Mr Marrumpeter's shop.

In Mr Marrumpeter's junk shop
There's everything under the sun.
There's raffia and rope
And a box of black soap,
There's dubbin. There's even an elephant gun
In Mr Marrumpeter's shop.

In Mr Marrumpeter's junk shop
If I had a couple of weeks,
I'd find all the things
Worth a fortune, like rings
And ivory and silver and priceless antiques
In Mr Marrumpeter's shop.

In Mr Marrumpeter's junk shop
I've seen an Arabian knife,
A map of the moon
And a left handed spoon,
A tap from Peru
And some Mexican glue,
The reins for a goat
And an Eskimo's boat,
A shark's fin, some creels,
A case of stuffed eels,
A buffalo bell
And some bagpipes as well,
Oh, I wish I could spend every day of my life
In Mr Marrumpeter's shop.

The Rainflower

Down in the forest where light never falls
There's a place that no one else knows,
A deep marshy hollow beside a grey lake
And that's where the rainflower grows.

The one silver rainflower that's left in the world,
Alone in the mist and the damp,
Lifts up its bright head from a cluster of leaves
And shines through the gloom like a lamp.

Far from the footpaths and far from the roads,
In a silence where no birds call,
It blooms like a secret, a star in the dark,
The last silver rainflower of all.

So keep close behind me and follow me down,
I'll take you where no one else goes,
And there in the hollow beside the grey lake,
We'll stand where the rainflower grows.

Two Friends

Jack

I said to Jack who must spend hours
Discussing politics with flowers:
"No plant can understand a man."
He smiled and answered: "Tulips can."

Tim

I know a man called Tricky Tim
Who says he taught a fish to swim
And says he taught a bird to fly.
He's teaching me to tell a lie.

Susannah

Susannah put her apron on,
"I'm a witch, I'm a witch," she said,
"And if you don't give me some diamonds,
I'll magic you into brown bread.
Who am I?" she asked her teddy.
"You're a witch," her teddy bear said.

Susannah put her slippers on,
"I'm a queen, I'm a queen," she said,
"And if you don't give me some rubies,
I'll chop all the curls off your head.
Who am I?" she asked her teddy.
"You're a queen," her teddy bear said.

Susannah put her nightdress on,
"I'm so tired, so tired," she said.
Then she yawned and took out her ribbons
And snuggled down into her bed.
"Who am I?" she asked her teddy.
"Susannah," her teddy bear said.

Uncle Ted's Tea

The table was laid and ready
For the visit of Uncle Ted,
When a horse looked in at the window
And whinnied a bit and said:

"I've come to make his excuses,
Your Uncle Ted can't come.
He fell off a chair last Thursday
And his ears have gone all numb,

But if those are crumpets I see
Behind that yellow cup,
I'll step inside and assist you
To eat the whole lot up."

Before we could speak or stop him
He was seated and tucking in,
He finished not only the crumpets
But the plates and the biscuit tin.

Then he smacked his lips and snickered
And went galloping out of the door,
Leaving us only some horse hairs
And his hoof prints on the floor.

A few minutes later the bell rang
And outside stood Uncle Ted
Smiling and stout on the doorstep,
"I hope I'm not late," he said.

We explained that the cupboard was empty,
That there wasn't a bite in the place.
"That horse has been here. I knew it!"
He cried going red in the face.

"Was he piebald and thin?" We nodded.
"That's Humphrey," he groaned in disgust.
"He promised to be my best friend,
A creature I could trust."

Then he turned away and left us,
Tut-tutting and shaking his head,
And he never comes round to tea now,
He comes to lunch instead.

So remember this little story,
There's a moral here, of course:
If you're asked out to tea and there's crumpets –
Don't ever tell a horse.

Cloudburst

There was a young cloud
Who wanted to rain.
Its cumulus mother said:
"What? Not again!
You're a stupid young cloud
Without any doubt,
Why didn't you say so
Before we came out?
It's supposed to be summer,
You'll just have to wait."
The little cloud answered:
"I can't. It's too late.
I'm so full I'm bursting,
I can't keep it in!"

And that's why our cricket match
Couldn't begin.

Gypsy Jill

She lived all alone in a little white house
On the top of a wild green hill.
She called us her children, although we weren't,
And we called her Gypsy Jill.

She was old and quick with a squint in one eye
And she stooped when her back was bad,
She kept a blind donkey and six black cats
And everyone said she was mad.

But she loved us and hugged us and made us wine
That tasted like best lemonade,
And she showed us where blackberries grew in the wood
And she knew where the fox cubs played.

And we loved her and hugged her and gave her flowers
And animals made out of bread,
And her bloomers were pink as the setting sun
When she leapfrogged or stood on her head.

She told us our futures in tea-leaves and cards
By the log fire's flickering light,
And we listened while shadows crept over the walls,
But our futures were always bright.

And she ran out to meet us . . . but now she's gone,
And the little white house has been sold.
They said she was mad. Well, if she was,
I hope I'm as mad when I'm old.

A Wild One

I heard him rustling about in the leaves
In a ditch at the edge of the wood.
He was square,
He was covered with hair,
He squeaked
And he sometimes leaked,
He could stand on one leg
And he sat up to beg
When I tickled his feathery tail,
His tummy was warm, his nose was cold,
I had no idea of his age,
His eyes were like buttons of burning gold
And I took him and built him a cage.

I papered it, polished it, planed it and put
A saucer of cream on the floor.
But he pined,
He sniffled and whined,
He sat
And his tail went all flat,
He hid in the straw
And he scratched at the door
Whenever I entered the room.
He cowered in a corner, crawled and crept,
He never once wanted to play,
He watered the cream with his tears when he wept
And his bright eyes began to turn grey.

I put him back under the leaves of the ditch
And he whisked away into the wood.
He was square,
He was covered with hair,
He squeaked
And he sometimes leaked,
He could stand on one leg
And he sat up to beg
When I tickled his feathery tail,
His tummy was warm, his nose was cold,
I had no idea of his age,
His eyes were like buttons of burning gold
And he didn't belong in a cage.

To Slim or Not to Slim

Uncle Slim said to Jim:
"You're too fat. You should slim."
"Who?" said Jim. "You," said Slim. "Me?" said Jim,
"I'm too fat?" "Yes," said Slim.
"I'm not fat," answered Jim,
"If I slim, I'll be thin, Uncle Slim."

At that moment Old Jim
Came along. "Jim," said Slim,
"Don't you think Jim should slim?" "What?" said Jim,
"Jim should slim?" "Yes," said Slim.
"No," said Jim, "not young Jim,
If Jim slims, he'll be slimmer than Slim."

"Who?" said Slim. "Slim," said Jim,
"Not you, Slim, but young Slim."
"Oh," said Slim, "Slim's much slimmer than Jim."
"Yes," said Jim, "Slim's too slim."
"Who's too slim, Jim?" said Jim.
"Slim's too slim, Jim," said Jim. "Yes," said Slim.

"Here he comes!" cried Old Jim.
"Who?" said Slim, "Not young Slim?"
"Yes," said Jim. "Hallo Slim." "Hallo Jim."
"Slim, Slim thinks Jim should slim."
"No, Jim's slim, aren't you, Jim?"
"Yes, Slim." "Yes," said Slim. "Jim, Slim, Jim, swim?"

My Dear Salooma

If stokes could eep and brombits feem,
If loods could sometimes sim,
If botter prooded empereem
And mooklets prooded im,

Then you and I would never sloom
Or dimp our lanterlay.
We'd follet ingles like the koom,
Keet feenings like the zay.

So let's take toot, let's roque and ven,
Let's bool a bit in twide.
There's only one quiss undergen
And soon will chimbers flide.

My dear Salooma, noostabar,
My dorna, friss and spree,
Come lide and limmer, mistaphar,
If stokes can't eep, can't we?

If Only

If I could be a grunting pig,
I would, and with my snout I'd dig
Deep down into the muddy ground
And deeper still until I found
A big potato, fat and sweet,
And then I'd eat and eat and eat
And when I'd eaten every bit
I'd fall asleep and dream of it:
That big potato, fat and round,
Deep down beneath the muddy ground.
Oh, with my snout I'd dig and dig. . .
If only I could be a pig.

How?

How did the sun get up in the sky?
– A billy goat tossed it up too high,
Said my Uncle.

How did the stars get up there too?
– They're sparks from the thunder-horse's shoe,
Said my Uncle.

And tell me about the moon as well.
– The moon jumped out of an oyster shell,
Said my Uncle.

And how did the oceans get so deep?
– I'll tell you tomorrow. Now go to sleep,
Said my Uncle.

A Corner of Bread

A magpie, a swan and a crow
Were arguing over a corner of bread,
"It's mine because I'm the smartest,"
The swaggering magpie said.

"You're common! It's mine," said the swan.
"My beautiful wings are whiter than snow."
"It's mine. I'm blacker than thunder
And stronger than you," said the crow.

They quarelled and fluttered and flapped.
The swan pecked the magpie, the crow pecked the swan,
Till they suddenly froze in amazement –
The corner of bread had gone!

The magpie, the swan and the crow
Stood goggling and gaping, unable to speak,
While high on a wire sat a sparrow
With a satisfied smile on its beak.

Can You Help?

Dear Reader,

Last night a man came to my door
With tearful eyes, all red and sore
And said: "I don't suppose you've seen
My parrot Joe; he's bottle green
With gold wings and a scarlet breast
And two white feathers in his crest.
He can't have flown too far away,
I only lost him yesterday."

I couldn't lie. I shook my head.
"But leave me your address," I said,
"And if I catch a glimpse of Joe
Or hear of him, I'll let you know."

He left with such a mournful look
I thought I'd try to use this book
To help. So if you ever spy
His friend Joe flashing through the sky,
Please get in touch with: Harry Brown,
10, Sawdust Gardens, Suppertown.

Thank you.

A Song without Music or Very Much Sense

In a menagerie in the zoo
A zebra, a sloth and a kangaroo
Were eating red cabbages out of a pot
When up jumped a hippo
And swallowed the lot.
O what a muddle, I've stepped in a puddle,
I'm off to Digereedoo.

In a metropolis in the sky
A beetle, a moth and a butterfly
Were tweaking the end of a thunder-cloud's nose
When up jumped a pigeon
And tickled their toes.
O what a muddle, I've stepped in a puddle,
I'm off to Digereedoo.

In an aquarium by the sea
A lobster, a lugworm, a sole and me
Were making some waterproof socks out of string
When up jumped a catfish
And started to sing:
O what a muddle, I've stepped in a puddle,
I'm off to Digereedoo.

The Wind

The wind runs rivers through the grass
And parts the clouds for birds to pass,
The wind dries shirts and skirts and socks
And wakes up sleepy weathercocks,
The wind sweeps cobwebs off the trees
And takes the scent of flowers to bees,
The wind lets flags and banners dance
And gives the dandy-clocks a chance,
And after snow and sleet and rain
The wind slips to the south again
To bring back spring without a fuss.
So, wind, who's such a friend to us,
Please tell me why, last Saturday,
You blew my five pound note away.

It

It's orange and green and purple and pink,
It's covered with flowers and fruit,
A thing like a catapult hangs from one end,
The other end's shaped like a boot.
It wobbles, it waggles, it quivers and nods,
It rocks like a ship in a gale,
In sunlight it sparkles, in moonlight it glows,
In mist it resembles a whale.
It rustles, it whimpers, it sighs in the night,
It groans when you're trying to sleep,
It squats on the shelf like a being from space
Or a creature dredged up from the deep.
What is it – this monster, this madness, this mess,
This home for three mice and a bat,
This stranger amongst us, this guest in the house?
Don't touch it! It's Granny's new hat!

Three Owls

Three owls were sitting in a tree,
Said one: "If two and one are three
And you are two as I can see
And we are three, then one is me!"
The other two said: "We agree."

Wizard

Under my bed I keep a box
With seven locks,

And all the things I have to hide
Are safe inside:

My rings, my wand, my hat, my shells,
My book of spells.

I could fit a mountain into a shoe
If I wanted to,

Or put the sea in a paper cup
And drink it up.

I could change a cushion into a bird
With a magic word,

Or turn December into spring,
Or make stones sing.

I could clap my hands and watch the moon,
Like a white balloon,

Come floating to my window-sill. . .

One day I will.

The Blue Room

My room is blue, the carpet's blue,
The chairs are blue, the door's blue too.
A blue bird flew in yesterday,
I don't know if it's flown away.

Be Careful

Be careful when you cross the road,
Be careful when you swim,
Be careful when you climb a tree,
Be careful when you crim.

I crimmed last week and look at me,
All coddled up in bed
With awful toothache in my ears
And heartburn in my head.

My nose is stiff, my tummy sings,
My legs have got the flu,
I can't read books without my eyes,
My neck keeps going: "Atchoo!"

The doctor gives me orange pills
To take when I'm asleep,
My knees won't touch my shoulder blades
And now my back's too steep.

My right hand's where my left should be,
My thumbs don't make a sound,
There's something pink inside my mouth,
My breath's the wrong way round.

So learn from me and my mistake:
Be careful when you swim
Or climb a tree, but most of all,
Be careful when you crim.

The Mandradum

Crouch down in a hollow tree,
Close your eyes and count to three,
When you look again you'll see
The Mandradum.

Watch his eyes dart to and fro,
Watch his curling whiskers glow,
Tell your troubles, then you'll know
The Mandradum.

When he speaks at first you'll hear
Thunder crashing in your ear,
Keep your courage, do not fear
The Mandradum.

Soon he'll soothe you, soon you'll find
Silver music in your mind
And your troubles far behind
The Mandradum.

When it's over just go out,
Do not wonder, do not doubt,
Never tell a soul about
The Mandradum.

George Mackenzie

Old George Mackenzie used to dance
With boxes on his feet,
He danced outside the playground wall,
He danced along the street.

He danced for statues in the park,
For gulls beside the sea,
He danced for scarecrows in the fields,
At night he danced for me.

I'd lie awake until I heard him
Thumping through the town,
His lullabying boxes calling:
Sleep now, settle down.

Till one dark day a car found George
And followed him about
And when he turned to dance for it
A grey-haired man got out.

Complaints had been received, he said –
A letter in his hand –
And George could either stop by choice
Or have his dancing banned.

George didn't speak when asked if he
Had anything to say,
Just kicked his boxes off and shuffled
Silently away.

And now at night I lie awake
And listen to the rain,
And cry for sleep and dreams and George
Who never danced again.

Say This as Fast as You Can

If you want to giggle and you want to sing
If your bed won't bounce and your legs won't spring
Pack a box in a bag and a bag in a box
Unlock those chains, unchain those locks
Go north, go south, go round and round
Till you hear the sight and you see the sound
Of wiggling and jiggling and clapping and clogs
It's Polly with her puppies, it's Molly with her moggs
It's pattering and chattering, smugglers and jugglers
Sally with her seals and her old Scotch reels
It's Clutterer's and Butterer's
Silly Nagger's, Nilly Wagger's
Old time, gold time, lollipops and lang syne
Shove a penny, love a penny
Yes dear! Up here!
Kiddies' and Siddie's and Grannies' and Nan's
Polka spotted, silver dotted, Flossie's old fans'
Everybody's, anybody's
Funnybody's, Moneybody's Circus! For who?
For you.
Phew!

Cooking

I do like cooking
I do like cooking,
With bubbly smells
All boiling up and hot,
With fruit and vegetables
In one giant pot.
I sometimes make up recipes
And try them on my Dad,
He's only been sick once or twice,
I can't be all that bad.

I did like cooking
I did like cooking,
But yesterday
I made a submarine
From prunes and leeks and eggs
And margarine.
I thought I'd put it on a shelf
For everyone to see,
But then my stupid little brother
Ate it for his tea.

I don't like cooking any more.

At Midnight

At midnight by the kitchen clock
A kettle on the shelf
Got tired of sitting silently
And whistled to itself.

A coffee pot took up the tune,
A ladle kept the beat,
Two saucepan lids joined in and crashed,
The cooker tapped its feet.

The floor mop asked the broom to dance,
They tangoed round and round
So gracefully it seemed their handles
Never touched the ground.

The tea cups rocked, the saucers rolled,
The mat flapped on the floor,
The fruit ski-ed down the draining board,
The blender whizzed: "Encore!"

But in the middle of the din
The quietest of the chairs
Whose back was to the wall cried: "Sh!
He's coming down the stairs!"

They all rushed madly round the room
To hook or shelf or drawer
And held their breath when Grandad's face
Peered slowly round the door.

He switched the light on, scratched his head
And yawned and tried to think,
Surely he hadn't left that orange
Floating in the sink.

And when he reached up for a mug
A sieve hung there instead.
"I must be getting old," he sighed
And shuffled back to bed.

The Rippling River

On the banks of the rippling river
With his toes in the water sat Jim,
When a trout popped its head up beside him
And invited him in for a swim.

After hiding his clothes in some bushes,
Jimmy dived in the river to play,
But he wasn't a very strong swimmer
And the current soon swept him away.

He was frightened. He couldn't touch bottom
And the water kept whirling him round,
So he called out for help, but his shouting
Disappeared in a much louder sound;

For around the next bend in the river,
Where the powerful current cut deep,
Hung a curtain of mist and behind it
Was a waterfall, roaring and steep.

Jimmy gulped and his mouth filled with water
And he spluttered and thought he might drown,
When he saw in the blue sky above him
A beautiful hand reaching down.

And the hand hovered over the water
And its fingers were soft on his arm
As it lifted him out of the river,
And it rocked him to sleep in its palm.

Jimmy woke in a circle of sunshine
On the banks of the sparkling stream,
And he rubbed his wet eyes as he wondered:
Did it happen or was it a dream?

My Little Dog

My little dog, old Loping Joe,
Was always chasing rabbits so
I hung a bell around his head
And now he chases me instead.

The Door

A white door in a hawthorn hedge –
Who lives through there?
A sorcerer? A wicked witch
With serpents in her hair?

A king enchanted into stone?
A lost princess?
A servant girl who works all night
Spinning a cobweb dress?

A queen with slippers made of ice?
I'd love to see.
A white door in a hawthorn hedge –
I wish I had a key.

A Forest by Night

When the sun goes down
And the bats come out
And the shadowy badger
Is moving about,

Then I sometimes hide
In my favourite tree
And watch all the creatures
Who can't see me:

The deer on the paths,
The mice in the leaves,
The foxes that tiptoe
As quietly as thieves.

A forest by night
Is an eerie place
Where a hole in the treetops
Can look like a face,

And I have to be brave
When a white owl shrieks
Or the branch that I'm sitting on
Suddenly creaks.

But when Mr Parks,
My teacher at school,
Makes me stand on a chair
And calls me a fool,

I wish I was back
In my favourite tree,
Just watching the creatures
Who can't see me.

The Song of a Mole

All I did this afternoon was
Dig, dig, dig,
And all I'll do tomorrow will be
Dig, dig, dig,
And yesterday from dusk till dawn
I dug, dug, dug.
I sometimes think I'd rather be
A slug, slug, slug.